About the Author

Israel L. Monzon Gonzalez is a Toronto based project coordinator and electrical engineering graduate who enjoys writing everything from poetry to sports articles. He is a devoted baseball and football fan who loves writing about and discussing sports. He is also a keen student of history and draws upon this knowledge to bring historical events and people to life through his poems. He strives to create pieces that make readers think of different aspects of life in new and interesting ways.

A Voice Cried Out in The Concrete Wilderness

Israel L. Monzon Gonzalez

A Voice Cried Out in The Concrete Wilderness

Olympia Publishers
London

www.olympiapublishers.com
OLYMPIA PAPERBACK EDITION

Copyright © Israel L. Monzon Gonzalez 2023

The right of Israel L. Monzon Gonzalez to be identified as author of this work has been asserted in accordance with sections 77 and 78 of the Copyright, Designs and Patents Act 1988.

All Rights Reserved

No reproduction, copy or transmission of this publication
may be made without written permission.
No paragraph of this publication may be reproduced,
copied or transmitted save with the written permission of the publisher,
or in accordance with the provisions
of the Copyright Act 1956 (as amended).

Any person who commits any unauthorized act in relation to
this publication may be liable to criminal
prosecution and civil claims for damage.

A CIP catalogue record for this title is
available from the British Library.

ISBN: 978-1-80439-010-8

First Published in 2023

Olympia Publishers
Tallis House
2 Tallis Street
London
EC4Y 0AB

Printed in Great Britain

Dedication

To my mother, father, and all others who in one way or another inspired me to take up the pen.

Foreword

What draws one to poetry? What moves a person to take up the pen and manipulate words in any number of creative ways? The answer differs from person to person and I shall not attempt to give any kind of general explanation for that very reason. Instead, I shall give you, the reader, my own personal reasons in this foreword because I want the ensuing collection of poems to serve as an overture into my mind in hopes that you too will feel inspired to 'come out of your shell'.

I have always had things to say about the world and its complexities. I also have much to say about other topics: sports, music, art, everyday life etc. However, venturing into the public domain with ideas, opinions and new art is often daunting. Questions always dog the mind. Is this work of importance? Am I sharing too much? Am I being inflammatory? Is this good enough? I am no different. I dithered for a long time on the pros and cons of embracing poetry and after much deliberation, I have taken the plunge and in your hands or on your screen is the product of said plunge. Its quality and merits I shall leave to your judgement but I take pride in having ventured into this space and encourage you to do likewise if you are having this same internal debate.

Throughout human history, progress has been driven by those who create. The pyramids of Giza, the Sistine Chapel, the airplane, the Strange Case of Dr. Jekyll and Mr. Hyde, and the litany of tech start-ups which exists today have a common thread, and that is they are the products of those who never fully abandoned their childlike impulses. Children are characterized by imagination, and the can-do attitude that accompanies it. Most of us view our childhoods with nostalgia for this very reason. To create is to be human and it is always worthwhile to create, regardless of how said creations are received. It gives life a sense of purpose and the more one does it, the better one becomes at one's chosen craft, and more importantly, the more secure one becomes in the sense that life is more than the 'get up, commute, work, commute, home, sleep' cycle in which so many of us trap ourselves. The goal of making this collection was to overcome my personal misgivings around embracing my own personal creative impulses. Reading this, I hope, will encourage you to pursue and win your own creative victory in the field of your choosing, and parlay that into more and more decisive creative victories in the future.

My little manifesto on embracing one's natural creativity aside, I want to answer the question 'Why poetry?'. What drew me was the idea of painting pictures with words; pictures of anything. Whether it is the chaotic workings of a mind under pressure, the terror of a man whose city is being sacked or the euphoria of a sports victory, the possibilities are endless. The seemingly endless ways in which people do this captivates me. In reading poetry and now in writing it, I have a new appreciation for the breathtaking malleability of words and the freedom that writing your own poetry brings. Without exaggerating, I can say it makes me feel all the much more alive. This in mind, I decided to embark on this poetic adventure.

What follows is the first chapter of my poetic adventure and the first serious attempt at winning the creative victory of which I spoke earlier. This foreword is my cordial invitation to join me on this adventure and walk this trail side by side with me as a friend. Hopefully, you will find yourself reflected in some of the ensuing passages and find this odyssey rewarding in some way. Without further delay, let us begin that adventure.

Section One: Humorous Poems

Introduction

Sometimes, in order to not despair of this world, one must laugh at it, or with it. The following poems are my attempt to do just that. Also, writing these poems allowed me to have fun with little tricks in word play or experiment with strange ideas or topics. Creating is childlike in its nature and humor is, in my view, the ultimate expression of this. I hope you get in a few good laughs reading through these poems, and I definitely do not mind if they come at my expense.

Laughter is good for the soul as they say, so it is rather appropriate that we start this poetic journey with a healthy dosage of laughter.

The ensuing poems are rather varied. Some deal with food, a topic we can all identify with. Others deal with the funnier side of social dynamics, and one with handwashing. I've taken a liking to coming at humor from different angles and frankly find it rewarding. I hope you the reader will as well.

The Most Muscular Mussel

The most muscular mussel of the sea

Herculean in his might was he

All the musselinas danced like ballerinas

Hoping to win his heart

He dazzled all with feats of strength

To keep toned he'd go to any length

Every day getting physical

His muscles feared by sharks and mussels alike

But one day they fished him out

To pull him out they needed men rather stout

For the Mr. Olympia of the sea the ultimate indignity

As the most muscular mussel of the dinner plate

With a side of brussels sprouts from Brussels

Mussels from Brussels on the menu tonight folks

Frank Incensed

Frank 'n' Sue had a good thing goin'

But then she left him high and dry

With only her scent of frankincense

Leavin' behind a Frank incensed

Frank and Franck were best of friends

But Franck had a taste for others' things

And took the last of the frankincense

Leavin' behind a Frank incensed

Frank 'n' "Scents" had good business

But one day the shopkeeper left

Sayin' "All outta frankincense"

Leavin' behind a Frank incensed

Geez Louise

Louise gets on up 'n' ready to roar

Cuz she's got the fam comin' o'er

She gets dressed and struts on o'er

To buy for dinner a little boar

She walks the streets in high heels with ease

Her black hair playin' in the wind

Her blue dress playin' in the wind

You know 'em boys be prayin' for a lil' breeze

Two o'clock and the fam's come on o'er

Louise knows she's in for a little bore

And a little boar

That she bought for twenty 'n' four

"Say Louise when's ya gettin' hitched?"

"Say yer lookin' a little chunky these days"

"Say yer lookin' a little bewitched"

"Geez Louise smile this ain't no sunny ways"

Louise gets mad 'n' storms on out

To pick her apples and pout

Her skin is hot and cold

You know her soul done got a little old

As she sits not sayin' a thing

A mockingbird comes out to sing

Then she stops 'n' thinks

Make 'em sing to shut 'em up she thinks

She cranks on the karaoke machine 'n' says

"Sing 'til ya can't speak no more," she says

And so they sing and sing

Sing, sing and sing some more

Their voices are shot and they steal away

Louise thinks "Geez Louise" there's always a way

Now the fam's gone and can't be seen

Louise done caressed that karaoke machine

A Germ for Jermaine

Cleanliness was a subject most germane to mama Germaine

Always telling little Jermaine to wash his little hands

But one day the little Jermaine didn't listen

And mama Germaine had a germy crisis on her hands

A germ for little Jermaine

And germs became a subject most germane

"Listen boy! Ya gotta listen!"

"Wash your hands or there'll always be a germ for Jermaine!"

The Countess of Inverness

The listless Countess of Inverness

Her days in bed she spent

No energy wherever she went

She wined and dined

Sighed and cried

As the days grew old and died

Oh the listless Countess of Inverness

The feckless Countess of Inverness

Strong character she lacked

The trust of her peers she lacked

She dithered and dithered

Blathered and blathered

As the days grew old and grandfathered

Oh the feckless Countess of Inverness

The careless Countess of Inverness

Loses all that she has

Is as organized as a horse's arse

She fumbled and jumbled

Bumbled and tumbled

As the days grew old and crumbled

Oh the careless Countess of Inverness

The Boring Poem

Joe's got the boring voice

Nun's got the boring holes

John's got the boring tools

CAT's got the boring machines

Elon's got the boring company

I's got the boring poem

The Terrible Tunes of Tumble Terrace

Wretched sounds flowed from Tumble Terrace

Owned by some very unknown heiress

She moved in with her pack of minstrels

Ruddy pack of drunkard minstrels

Who could barely play a lick or two

Drunk before there was morning dew

They would get up on the rooftop

One would shout "Alright from the top!"

And terrible tunes would sound from Tumble Terrace

Hear the terrible tunes of Tumble Terrace

Brainchild of the Tumble heiress

Drunken songs of Tumble Terrace

Pack your patience if you walk on by

They'll kill you but you will not die

Cognac flows so freely in the house of Tumble Terrace

Drunken music fills the halls

You would think that you're in Paris

In some fancy Versailles balls

The only tears there come from laughter

Or from naked annoyed anger

Because the songs are just so terrible

Hear the terrible tunes of Tumble Terrace

Brainchild of the Tumble heiress

Drunken songs of Tumble Terrace

Pack your patience if you walk on by

They'll kill you but you will not die

Hear the terrible tunes of Tumble Terrace

Brainchild of the Tumble heiress

Drunken songs of Tumble Terrace

Pack your patience if you walk on by

They'll kill you but you will not die

Unable To Communicate With Server

Unable to communicate with server

Please try again later

Communication down with server

Okay, see you later alligator

No unread emails suits me just fine thanks

Just like a desert suits a Berber

And money suits the banks

Unable to communicate with server

Unable to communicate with server

She seems a little grumpy today

Said hello but she didn't answer

I hope she had a blessed day today

Seems upset like the desert deprived Berber

Guess her dessert deserted her today

And a lack of sweetness sure does hurt

Unable to communicate with server

Section Two: Historical Poems

Introduction

If there is any subject that has captured and kept my attention wherever life may take me, it is history. Peering into the past offers us insight into and understanding of the world in which we live today. Events taking place today can be traced back as the culmination of a series of past actions and events. Doing this also allows one to attempt predicting future events, no psychic powers involved. In order for us to know who we are today, we must know who we were. History and the figures who color it, are of great importance to me for these reasons.

But the question arose of how to make sharing historical facts engaging. Historical texts can be onerous. They can also sometimes dehumanize history, and detach us from the emotions that the people involved in historical events must have felt. My idea was to see if I could use poetry to make moments or people in history come alive in a way that is engaging and emotionally investing in whatever way is appropriate. The ensuing poems are the results of this endeavor and they cover wars, uprisings, protest movements and historical figures such as composers, athletes, philosophers and kings.

Black is the Night

Black is the night

T'is might that makes right

City's under siege tonight

Never again to see the light

The land is ravaged

The towns pillaged

No respite envisaged

They've made it here

The city we hold dear

Its end is near

Black is the night

Moonless is the night

Only shivers of fright tonight

T'is Tisha B'Av tonight

The stomach's growl

The stench is foul

Only singer is a lonely owl

The temple is burning

Incense and bodies are burning

OUR NATION IS BURNING!

Black is the night

Woe to us this night

The prophets were right

What is wrong is not right

The Holy City is captured

The king is captured

His eyes from his face raptured

People carted off to a distant land

Guided by a heavy hand

Babylon ain't no Promised Land

Black is the night

Jacob is not pitied tonight

Not pitied tonight

Black is the night

Lo ruhamah, lo ruhamah, LO RUHAMAH!

Shouted a walking carcass at me

His crazed look frightening me

Summer has passed and we are not saved

WE ARE NOT SAVED!

We are not saved

Black is the night

Our leader is blind tonight

Our Lord is silent tonight

Black is the night

Zedekiah damn your eyes!

Did you not listen when Jeremiah said to open them?

How could you have been so blind?

Now your sons and mine are dead!

OUR NATION IS DEAD!

All because you were blind

But I bet you can see clearly now

Black is the night

Black is the night

Black is the night!

BLACK IS THE NIGHT!

The Man of Twelve Tongues

The man of twelve tongues knows it all

Only hit .220 but that's also his IQ

Caught and threw from spring till fall

Then the OSS came calling

Moe had a brand-new job

Snapping pics for Uncle Sam

Sailed the Pacific with Ruth and Gehrig

In 1934 it was Tokyo calling

Hirohito never knew, oh damn!

War broke out and Moe got a call

Germans be working on an atom bomb

We stop 'em now or Olympus might fall

So Moe tracked down bad ol' Werner

Found him brooding on his uncertainty

Gotta kill him that's a certainty

But Moe was no killer

And the Nazi lived to be punked by a Jew

Not so superior after all

And Moe became the wisest of Americans

The man of twelve tongues sure knows it all

The Snake of Actium

The waters of Actium decided Rome's fate

As boats sped aimlessly past their orders

To the losers one last consolation

Enter the snake of Actium

Its beauty is in its poison to the noble Roman

No greater closeness to heaven than its fangs

It takes Antony and his dreams of empire with it

Then it goes where all men dream to go

The breast of Cleopatra

And kills her dead!

Nuts!

Winter: 1944-45

GIs freezin' their nuts off at Bastogne

Germans comin' on like bees outta their hive

No hope for resupply

Weather outside: Frightful

Morale: Wonderful

Herr Lüttwitz writes a letter

'To the American commander:

Gig's up! Surrender now!

It's for the better.

Signed – the German commander'

"Aww nuts! They got us surrounded"

Says McAuliffe – then he thinks

"What else to say?" he thinks

'To the German commander:

NUTS!

Signed – the American commander'

"Was dost dies mean?" asks Lüttwitz

"Means 'go to hell' mein general"

Lüttwitz thinks, "Aww nuts"

The 101st will surely kick our butts

And so they did

After seven days of fury

Nuts!

Blenheim

The bloody battle of Blenheim

In 1704 was fought

O'er the crown of Spain t'was fought

Marlborough 'n' his red coats

Must've had 'em mornin' oats

For they kicked the French good in the rear

At the bloody battle of Blenheim

The Ire of the Irish

The ire of the Irish burned brightly

For many a year treated wrongly

The heat became hit on Easter Sunday

The whole damn thing ground to a halt that day

Sunday ain't no fun day in Dublin town

1916: the world seems irredeemably torn down

Big plans being made over a glass of whiskey

Or two or three

Guns be firing on you: one, two, three

Blood paints the streets a red quite dusky

But neither side of the Irish Sea can find the key

So it's a bullet or two or three for you and me

Celtic fire burns fiery green

For the English were quite a bit mean

Cannons and small guns flashed

Shells into people crashed

These were the republic's birth pains

Killing and dying under cold April rains

The ire of the Irish boiled over

Connolly and Pearse said, "Rebel, rebel, come on over!"

"Take your gun and fight them off!"

But British fury eventually bumped them off

Yet nothing could being the people back on side

The ire of the Irish would not subside

Beyond the Pale

1914

The bells ring and ring

The songbirds don't sing

The world's at war

It's gone to hell

The lion, the bear and the eagle roar

Hence the church bells toll and toll

Look! A race to the sea can't you see

'Murica sees but leaves 'em be

Out east, the Ruskie bear advances west

But lo, at Tannenberg is second best

T'is all futile my boys, t'is all futile

But t'is o'er the top my boys, o'er the top

And as the bullets whiz on by you'll ask yourself why

But let not your courage fail

That would be beyond the pale

1915

The clouds turn a sickly yellow

Sure ain't no mellow yellow

'Em boys be turnin' pale

Feelin' fire in their lungs

Shortly after they kick the pail

Ypres is a meat grinder

Gallipoli too is a meat grinder

The Syrian desert is an orgy of death

A million plus 'll no longer draw a breath

T'is all futile my boys, t'is all futile

But t'is o'er the top my boys, o'er the top

And as the bullets whiz on by you'll ask yourself why

But let not your courage fail

That would be beyond the pale

1916

There's a bloodbath at Verdun

Mother Earth, she's come undone

First of July means fire on the Somme

Sky's pierced by the chilling screams of mom

Proud ships are burned and sunk at Jutland

And in the end, victory belongs to England

Can man really be so cruel?

Going forward is this the rule?

What will is there to live?

When death is all man has to give?

T'is all futile my boys, t'is all futile

But t'is o'er the top my boys, o'er the top

And as the bullets whiz on by you'll ask yourself why

But let not your courage fail

That would be beyond the pale

1917

The Russian bear's gettin' hangry

Fightin' men are gettin' angry

An ominous figure emerges from the Finland station

Revolution's 'bout to grip the nation

In the Holy City flies the Union Jack

At Vimy, Currie plans a successful attack

The maple leaf flies and a nation is born

Into a world all torn

Into the fray comes Uncle Sam

Wilson after the telegram gives a damn

The muds of Passchendaele claim many a man

A battle more furious than the revenge of Queen Anne

France's finest are in mutiny

Puttin' their officers under lots of scrutiny

T'is all futile my boys, t'is all futile

But t'is o'er the top my boys, o'er the top

And as the bullets whiz on by you'll ask yourself why

But let not your courage fail

That would be beyond the pale

1918

Hunger grips Vienna's regal streets

Around Europe not too many eats

"To hell with Karl and Czeta," the Viennese shout

As in Europe the old order makes its way out

The baron falls from the sky like lightning from heaven

Of his lives he finally expended all seven

At Amiens, Ludendorff has his blackest day

But a hundred days pass before there can be laughing and gay

In a lonely baggage train the madness ends

Eleven, eleven, eleven, and the hostility ends

T'is all futile my boys, t'is all futile

But t'is o'er the top my boys, o'er the top

And as the bullets whiz on by you'll ask yourself why

But let not your courage fail

That would be beyond the pale

1919

The war is over yes it is

Go home and hug your family

If the Spanish Lady hasn't already

Live with your wounds soldier

Both seen and unseen

Dare to live a normal life if you can

And let not your courage fail

That would be beyond the pale

The Last Lament of King Saul

I count the stars at night hoping to forget

Thousands surround me but I'm alone

In the midst of the cold and bitter night

Shivering in abject fright

God and Sam have said I'm on my own

And that my comeuppance I will get

I once reigned supreme in the land of Israel

Till one day David's star began to shine

And giants he did kill

I have killed of our enemies thousands

But he, tens of thousands

And my world tumbled downhill

And slowly he took all that was mine

And my kingdom went to hell

Like an arrow from Jonathan's bow I touched the sky

Only to crash ignominiously to earth

I went from herder to king to a man condemned

Accursed by the prophet and God himself

Facing my tribulations all by myself

My sons and these thousands also condemned

To be one again with the earth

Yet not a single brave man dares ask why

In the distance the Philistines sleep tight

In a land not theirs but no longer ours

I will conquer or be a head fixed to their gate

But a prisoner? Never!

And as a martyr I'd live forever

My absurd fate I do hate

But I count down the hours

As my destiny approaches and all is right

To the boy with the sling, my kingdom

For it is God's will

It is written

That I should be smitten

But I will remain on that hill

Mount Gilboa is now my kingdom

Frau Schopenhauer

Frau Schopenhauer was the best companion

Better than any human could ever be

Her fluffiness filled the thinking man's heart

For she alone understood the world was will

Blind, insatiable, metaphysical will

And though the youngsters laughed

And the has-beens scorned

She never left his side

And most devoted a student in pessimism she remained

The most beautiful of poodles

Prominent in the doodles of the thinking man's mind

Money he shall bequeath so she wants not

For to the pessimist she taught the meaning of love

Eddie Gaedel Comes to Bat

Now batting… pinch hitting for Saucier

Number one eighth

Eddie… GAEDEL!

"What? Where'd you get this guy?"

"Has Veeck lost his mind?"

"Browns are terrible but…"

"Three feet 'n' eight inches tall?"

Umpire says, "Is this joke?"

"No," says Skip, "Papers are signed"

"Alight, PLAY BALL!" the ump says

The Detroit nine recoil in laughter

The St. Louis nine do just the same

On the mound good ol' Bobby Cain

Get his sign 'n' winds 'er up

The pitch…

BALL ONNNEE!

Gaedel ahead in the count

Cain gets set and deals again

BALL TWWWOOOO!

"Dammit Cain! Quit laughin' 'n' throw a strike"

Cain breathes in 'n' tries again

BALL THREEEEE!

"He's a patient little runt"

"Take all the way Eddie!"

Cain's rollin' over 'n' can't even breathe

But it's heave-ho, gotta get one in there

Theeee piiitch…

BALL FOUURRR!!!! Take yer base!

Eddie walks to first

He's done his deed

Veeck'll be a happy man indeed

Let's go Browns and…

Aaawww, they're running for the little guy

Exit stage right then Eddie

You're now immortal

Little American hero take yer bow

The Ballad of Gregor MacGregor

Good ol' General Gregor Macgregor o' clan Gregor Master swindler of the Scots

'll rip the bloomin' bloomer of yer wife if he's got the hots

Christmas child of an East India man

First saw the light within the walls of Glengyle

Destined to get through life with a lotta guile

All hail the good ol' Gregor Macgregor

Good ol' General Gregor Macgregor o' clan Gregor

Served king 'n' country through many Iberian days

Irked a good many in many ways

Had a seven year fling with Maria Bowater

But what to do after the death of the Mrs.

Head to 'zuela! The land of the lovely misses!

All hail the good ol' Gregor Macgregor

Good ol' General Gregor Macgregor o' clan Gregor

'Sir Gregor' arrived in Caracas to a great rumble

In stating credentials he was anything but humble

The dashing Scot tied the Royalists into a knot

Vexed many from Cartagena to Florida to Porto Bello

Vexations which made many for his death bellow

All hail the good ol' Gregor Macgregor

Good ol' General Gregor Macgregor o' clan Gregor

Hail the Cazique of Poyais!

Lots of fertile land in Central America o' yay

He'll sell ya land for cheap 'n' buy yer soul for even cheaper

Get yer patch along the Mosquito Coast

From the Scot who makes many a boast

All hail the good ol' Gregor Macgregor

Good ol' General Gregor Macgregor o' clan Gregor

Bolivar 'n' a million others wanted him dead

But the sneaky Scot was never gonna lose his head

When he heard that Simon was first to kick the bucket

He returned to 'zuela to trample on his grave

And was made a general for the republic he did once save

All hail the good ol' Gregor Macgregor

Good ol' General Gregor Macgregor o' clan Gregor

Leading scoundrel of the Scots

Who tied many a brain into a million knots

Evading pitchforks till he died in '45

And the Caracas elite lined up to say farewell

All things told his end was rather swell

All hail the good ol' Gregor Macgregor

Confession of a Parisian Lobster

I lobster

Property of the greatest gymnopedist

Monsieur Satie

Most renowned of artists

Whose vexations are written for piano

Whose hammer shields him from harm

I walk the arrondissements with you rope in rope

Oh man of twelve grey suits

Collector of umbrellas

Enemy of the sun

Impart your gnosis to me

With every note you play

Your haunter of the Chat Noir

Who keeps tall buildings in his drawer

Je te veux

I lobster, love you

Monsieur Satie

The Return of Hell

No sight more fearsome than that of the angry Prussian

Like a loathsome plague he makes his way east

His pride still injured from the black day at Amiens

His fury spares not even the least

The Tricolor trampled upon

The European continent rendered servile

The Leningrader hungry

But the man with the cigar will never bow

From the machine guns a rain of death

From the ghetto unanswered calls for help

From the clerics complicit silence

From the new world hope for deliverance

The apocalypse has come again

Blood spills profusely

Fifty million souls sacrificed on the altar of human cruelty

Fire rains from the heavens

The time of Jacob's trouble is here

The largest of pogroms

His wounds will number six million

But he will survive and make it home

Hell is here

It announced itself with a few shots on Danzig

The four horsemen just rode into town

But humanity will survive though scarred forever

Dear Jacob

Dear Jacob

It's been a long, long slog

After a long road traveled and all the pain

At last you've made it home

I heard Nebuchadnezzar sent you packing

Seventy years of waiting

Loving, hating and praying

Rode back with Cyrus when Babylon took a sacking

You went back to a house no longer yours

Had to give Alex, Ptolemy and Seleucus VIP tours

But when Antiochus made you treat him like a god

He got the Judean hammer blow courtesy almighty God

Dear Jacob

Heard you had it good for about eighty years

Had oil for a day and that lasted for eight

And or the briefest of moments everything was great

Then came the Romans to make you shed all them tears

Titus cut, burnt and stabbed you all them years

And when you sought at last to avenge your name

Hadrian took your fame, your game and even your name

Heard you took to wandering the earth some

Clocked more miles than Voyager One and then some

Saw the world but they didn't like you

Tried to burn you so you could stop being you

The world got smarter, faster and smaller

New found knowledge had them feeling a little taller

You thought your lot had improved they say

But they gave you no love just the same

They accused you of running the show

In spite of having little room to grow

Nobody ever kept you in the know

But did you know you control when we're getting snow

You showed love

They ain't never show nothing back to you

Even accused you of not having their back

But in the end it was they who stabbed you in back

Dear Jacob

I heard the Germans did you dirty

Said you were subhuman or something

Left you for dead and nobody did nothing

Gassed, starved, beaten and shot

Cried for help but it was all for naught

Six million wounds Hitler gave you

Yet you stand tall and he ain't breathin'

Dear Jacob

Enough was enough so you went home

Five armies came like they were marching on Rome

Two weeks at most was the prognosis

But in a year you beat into them a little gnosis

In '48 they came and you laid down the law

In '67 they came back for some more flayin'

So you punked them in six like you was The Klaw

And again in '73 even though they caught you prayin'

Many say the land doesn't belong to you

But even the desert blooms when it sees you

Man it's like everything came back to life

When they saw you coming through the door

It's been a long tough road

Dear Jacob

So glad you're still alive

So proud to call you a friend man

Long life to you – L'chaim

2019

The youth of the world take up arms

They learn that they have rights for which they must fight

They know that the future is cradled in their right arms

From all walks of life they stand tall

Well prepared to lose it all

For what is right they will fight

Aux armes les citoyens, aux armes!

From Iran to Venezuela to Bolivia to Hong Kong

Young hearts can do no wrong

We will not stand in line

2019 is our 1989

Shoot if you must but remember one thing

We won't retreat and we won't surrender

Even as we hear the bullets ring

We will keep marching

And every fight you pick will have its contender

O youth of the world remember one thing

Aux armes les citoyens, aux armes

From Iran to Venezuela to Bolivia to Hong Kong

Young hearts can do no wrong

We will not stand in line

2019 is our 1989

As our world goes to hell all torn asunder

In the distance you'll hear a faint rolling thunder

That's the shout of a whole generation

With a new explanation

As Scott Mackenzie said

And no matter how many get shot in the head

Many more will rise from down under

Aux armes les citoyens, aux armes

From Iran to Venezuela to Bolivia to Hong Kong

Young hearts can do no wrong

We will not stand in line

2019 is our 1989

Milena

He'd trade the worlds he makes for laughter

He'd give them all to laugh with you

He knows his load is very heavy

His saddest eyes do tell you so

Milena, the farthest shining star, Milena

Good old Franz sure loves you so

Milena

His hand does tremble to the rhythm

With which ink stains the page he writes

He paints the love with which he loves you

In black and white upon his page

Milena, you are the only cause, Milena

For which hunger's not his art

Milena

His pen caresses white-ish paper

The way he'd love to do with you

From his despair you are his shelter

His ray of sunshine in the rain

Milena, he'd go from man to bug, Milena

If it meant spending life with you

Milena

He'd brave the judgements of his father

If he could share a grave with you

He'd sell insurance gladly

If you'd involve yourself with him

Milena, would you hop right in, Milena

Into the depths of his abyss

Milena

You are the force moving his fingers

Though he wastes away in pain

He'd swallow whole his pain

If you would remain his muse

Milena, what power do you have, Milena

That the dead remain alive

Milena

The 2021 Song

You've been in prison for one year

Wasting away in your broken dreams

As life switched into another gear

You're breaking down like a Chinese rocket

Dropping erratically back to earth

Who knows where you will land

Or how much of you will burn

Your mind is swirling without control

Far away from here

Like an Italian dervish who just wants to see you dance

It doesn't care if you understand

Death floats all around though you can't see

It's been a year since you've a smile

It's been long since you've walked a mile

Cold wars are turning hot

Water is worth its weight in gold

No thought for the souls they've sold

Or the lines drawn upon your face

Your mind is swirling without control

Far away from here

They say a probe on Mars caught it in its sights

It says 'to hell with Earth'

Every Day the Lightning Falls

Lightning on a summer's day

Rocks the mountains high

I stare at the sky all grey

All left out to dry

Rumbles in clouds get loud

Rattling the structures proud

Cannons in the heavens flash

While I on Earth do crash

Every day the lightning falls

Rumbles fill the market stalls

And amidst the pouring rain

Behold the dancing grain

Hot winters make for cold springs

Said the shaman with three rings

Not sure if the peace pipe spoke

Or the man behind the smoke

In the warrior's painted face

Lie the wounds of past disgrace

The hunger on his worried eyes

Grows as the last bison dies

Every day the lightning falls

It rumbles through the empty halls

Of the stomach rarely fed

Of a people wanted dead

It rumbles through the forlorn plains

Like the growling belly in its pains

They say the Big Bear's fallen dead

Reservation life filled him up with dread

The rebels giving up their guns

The land no longer for their sons

The thunder growls upon their lands

Strangers now to their hands

He's a Rebel

He holds no gun in hand

He's leading no merry, merry band

He's a rebel

He's a lonesome rebel

He's in search for some portal to a new dawn

He's always gotta have the light on

He's a rebel

He's a lonesome rebel

He stares insistently at a distant galaxy

He's in communion with the old man and the sea

He's a rebel

He's a lonesome rebel

He's occupied with sizing infinities

With directions and with cardinalities

He's a rebel

He's a lonesome rebel

He's living in a world that they can't understand

He's a charlatan they say throughout the land

He's a rebel

He's a lonesome rebel

Section Three: Romantic Poems

Introduction

Throughout history, a good amount of art has had the common thread of love. Most of humanity spends a fair amount of time fantasizing about falling in love, being in love, or reeling from the ill effects of love gone wrong. Top 40 radio today and in the past has been saturated with songs having romantic themes. Paintings, poems, stories etc. to celebrate love, describe the feeling of being in love and so forth. No poetry collection therefore would be complete without a few pieces on the subject.

After all, what facet of the human experience can elicit such radically different emotions? From the impotence of a platonic love which only exists in the mind, to the exhilaration of being in love, it seems to influence us in such radically different, but similarly profound ways. Furthermore, we are all products of some form of love between two people, making love an inescapable part of ourselves. This alone makes love worthy of the lopsided attention it receives and worth exploring further in this collection. I hope to have done this most important and cherished facet of the human experience justice.

The Woman of Many Colors

Her rainbow silhouette streaks brightly in the night oh so dark

So irresistible is she though your prospects with her are oh so stark

Her red dress glimmers in the starless night

As she smiles her pearly white teeth set the world alight

She beckons for your presence with a flick of her hand

In your stupor you are deaf to the playing of the band

Her emerald green eyes invite you to partake in her inner world

Then she watches you writhe in pain as she withholds from you this world

Running her finger through her crimson lip as you thirst to know more

Her peachy skin radiates in delight knowing she's anything but a bore

She paints you yellow with the sickness of love

Each stroke of her black hair reminding you she's not quite the purest dove

But you don't care how many times she leaves you blue

To have her with what little you have you'll make due

It doesn't matter if she treats you to many a slight

She remains that pleasant haunting in your greyest nights

She is the woman of many colors that paints your existence

But she'll always elude you no matter the level of your persistence

She always does

And she'd do the same to us

A Tongue Well Tied

Consumed am I by the recurring vision

That of her crimson painted smile flashing at me

Yes dear friend, that is my condition

I am tortured through my own volition

One look at her and me

And I wish that we were we

But she won't know by me

That's my premonition

For mine is a tongue well tied

I'd say I told her how I feel

That my love for her is real

But I would have lied

My tongue is tied

She's a beautiful creature

A beautiful creature with every desirable feature

My dreams are dreamt and my poems written

Which she'll never read

Our story remains unwritten

And what a whale of a tale it is

Where happiness is hers and his

But condemned to vagaries remains unwritten

For mine is a tongue well tied

I'd say I told her how I feel

That my love for her is real

But I'd have lied

My tongue is tied

Jacob

Alone and shivering in the moonless night

Some Jacob traverses Canaan in search of his Rachel

Trapped in his bar less prison his mind takes flight

And a ladder appears which the angels do climb

Can he grab hold before Esau drags him to hell?

That Esau called the passage of time

As he traverses his desert he believes himself to have found her

He'll give seven years to the man in white for her

And another seven if he gets a rotten deal

Though his stomach pangs for lack of a meal

This sailor believes himself to have found his port

Hoping to have not been strung along for sport

Shall she lead him by the hand up the ladder to heaven?

Or shall she smash it into a million pieces?

Condemning him to remain in the abyss

She does the latter and 'poof' goes the ladder

Surely Esau will hack him to pieces

As the massage his feet the snakes do surely hiss

And so he finds himself a man condemned

To a life of wrestling with angels

Who'll rack his body and change his name

For this Jacob a brand-new ballgame

He is a man condemned

To no heavens and a million hells

The Eyes of a Showgirl

"Come with me!" her defiant eyes scream

Those of that show girl that makes you dream

Those liquid dreams of yours that you dream

"Fill my heart with wonder tonight"

"Do it baby, you know it's right"

And you feel the tingle in your belly

That serpent of old of yours stands to attention

Awakened by the sweet fragrance of lust

It knows damn well that it surely must

And as your legs slowly turn to jelly

You know you're feeling just a bit of tension

"What are you waiting for?" her defiant eyes ask slitheringly

"You know you want to love me tonight"

"Wrap your arms around my bosom just right"

"Let our toes dance with each other this night"

You prepare to act and look at her embracingly

You undress her in your mind

Because you know she's your kind

"Take me to heaven," those defiant eyes of her say

"Love me till our bodies secrete their passions"

"And keep my fire burning till the end"

None the Wiser

She was seeing another man

Never got wind of it man

Thought what we had was for real

Thought we would make it for real

But I didn't know she would betray me

Guess that's how it is she don't care about me

Hurts to know that I was none the wiser

Hard to find out that you're somebody's fool

Could have gave me the boot

But instead she played me like a lute

She was probably speaking in signs

Never quite read all the signs

How was I fooled for so long

Her line of fools must be long

But I didn't know she would betray me

Guess that's how it is she don't care about me

Hurts to know that I was none the wiser

Hard to find out that you're somebody's fool

Could have gave me the boot

But instead she played me like a lute

Cold Fire

It used to be that nothing could keep us apart

But time has broken us down

Torn our love to the ground

I don't even recognize you any more

Our love used to burn white hot

But it's a cold, cold fire now

It used to be that we would hit the park

But work means I'm never at home

You sit there all alone

Watching the years go by

Our love used to burn white hot

But it's a cold, cold fire now

It used to be that we worked to live

But now we live to work

We kiss the screens

But never each other's lips

Our love used to burn white hot

But it's a cold, cold fire now

We've crossed the Rubicon darling

And there's nothing left to do

We've had our golden age

And now we're on the decline

Our love used to burn white hot

But it's a cold, cold fire now

Lost and Never Found

I glanced across and was confronted with a mystery

I want a future with this creature in front of me

Though I'm ignorant of her history

Anything it takes to have a dance with her I will do

A flick of her hair sets me in motion

The crossing of her legs causes within me a commotion

Not even a few minutes and in my heart a gape

I'm in a prison from which I desire no escape

Within a candle begins to burn

Butterflies flutter gently within my entrails

I embark on a journey with no return

Off I go now to explore her unseen trails

And I wander into her forest to be lost and never found

With those defiant green eyes she challenges me

Dares me to be her knight in shining armor

To be of them all the greenest arbor

But alas knights are things of a bygone age

All I am is one who works for a modest wage

But in a world full of bore a little laughter is all she's after

So I play the clown

I change who I am and play her game

Until I get to where I barely know my name

And I wander into her forest to be lost and never found

I stare intently at her eyes and dip into her ocean blue

As she disappears into the night I feel a little bit blue

My mind feeds on the phantoms of my illusion

That our story will have a happy conclusion

I wish for her to let me make her garden bloom

Anything else for me now would be certain doom

I settle in and across the window flies a dove

As I dream sweet dreams of her love

And I wander into her forest to be lost and never found

What Is Love

A coming together of two souls

Who see nothing but each other

And give each other everything

Though they may have nothing

Answer? What is love

Two fires burning through the rain

Two hands held firmly no matter the pain

Sleepless nights wondering where the other must be

Though neither considers betrayal to any degree

Answer? What is love

Two vessels sailing a sea of their own

To a port from which only they hail

And through the roughest seas they continue to sail

Without care if the families disown

Answer? What is love

A mystery religion followed by two

Where neither would ever break faith

Clinging together in the morning dew

The primary article of their faith

Answer? What is love

Deathly agony should the other suffer

Two lives worth living only in concert

Each with their array of enchantments

Spells which only work on each other

Answer? What is love

Silent Beauty

Oh silent beauty look my way

Show me your smile and turn my night into day

Let your voice sing so I can hear the heavenly host

Oh silent beauty tease with the scent of your perfume

Why do you share my look of doom and gloom

Let us heal each other and make ourselves whole

Oh silent beauty thrill me with your touch

And no, I do not ask for too much

Let us teach each other to fly tonight

Oh silent beauty mark me as yours with your kiss

If we're together there'll be nothing amiss

Let me see your eyes and lose all sense of time

Oh silent beauty I love you so

Take me by the hand and let us go

And dance our blessed dance tonight

Inescapable

As I oscillate between asleep and awake

The taste of your lips lingers on my mind

The tender melody of your voice sings of us

Far away a star mimics the sparkle of your eyes

And a certain warmth overcomes me

As if your body lay draping mine

Turning winter into spring as if by magic

The rhythm of your beating heart I hear

As my spirit dances to its beat

Though far away you may be you are near

I can feel your loving vibes

Far as you may be

And every contour of your figure I can sketch

No matter how many days go by

I can't help but draw you in my mind

You're always there even if you're not

You're inescapable

Not that I care to set myself free

A Polyglot in Love

Senza parole

You leave me speechless

Amore mio

There is sunshine in your smile

That breaks the clouds into pieces

There is fire in your lips

Which burn so tender in the night

Quemame con tu fuego cariño mio

Alumbra mi noche con tu luz

Your hand leaves stardust in its wake

As it trudges through my nervous skin

The goosebumps are every particle in me

Reaching out to be a part of you

Tu es la vedette des mes rêves

Et mes nuits ont saveur de toi mon amour

Ti voglio bene

Ti penso amore

E io amo te

Oh the excitement when your hair brushes my arm

How all the storms inside grow calm

At the smell of your perfume

Que locura es esta que me haces sentir amor

Que el tiempo se para al besar tus labios

La noche se hace tierna con rozar tu piel

Me dejas sin palabras amor

You leave me scrambling for a language in which to say

How beautiful you are

T'es ainsi belle mademoiselle

Et je t'aime sans remède

On Platonic Love

I casted a gaze upon the faces in the crowd

Behold!

My sweetest blessing and my foulest curse mixed into one

As her eyes met mine for the first time

Endowed was I

With a flake of heaven and a sliver of hell

The sublimity of a thought mixed with the purity of the knowledge

In my mind she was mine

But in actuality she belonged to another

In the darkest recess of my brain life is beautiful

But amidst the colors of the world in which I live

A deathly emptiness exists of that which could never be

But I am content

All is well

For at least in this inner world foreign to my fellow man

There exists a love so pure and perfect

Immune to the sands of time

And the ravages of human existence

Wanting Her

It's a dream

An impossible dream

It's an illusion made of heart and mind

Yes reality is so unkind

You see she already has her man

And he loves her so

And she loves him so

She would not trade for any other man

I know that I am foolish for wanting her

That I am a fool for loving her

When she has no more love to give

But I will love her still

So long as we both shall live

It's a sin

A delectable sin

It's a delusion made of heart and soul

Yes true love can be so cruel

You see not all hearts can be filled

And they run on empty

Till the glass of life runs empty too

I'm glad her heart with joys is filled

I know that I am foolish for wanting her

That I am a fool for loving her

When in another man's dreams she'll live

But I will love her still

So long as we both shall live

Love and I

The days go by

I cry and I don't know why

It could never be

So far as I can see

That she could be with me

So why do I torture myself

With those sonnets of love upon my shelf

Love is not meant for me

It could never be

So far as I can see

Why do I feel her in my arms

Smell her perfume on my pillow

Hear her heartbeat on my chest

Why is she still my dream

When I never got to be her nightmare

It makes no sense

And never will

Where There is a Woman

Where there is a woman there is a song

Which sings of rebirth

A continuation of that which is human

A giving of life

From a giving wife, a giving mother, a giving daughter

Where there is a woman there is a letter

Written to bear witness to all she brings to bear

Her love, her warmth and shelter

The ember of life and love which through her

The healing touch and speech of her shelter

Where there is a woman there is a candle

Standing tall and burning bright

On those around her shining light

Through the thunder and the rain

It continues to burn with the flame of her life

Section Four: Contemplative Poems

Introduction

We humans as a norm spend much time lost in thought. These thoughts vary widely. At any given time, we may find ourselves confronting our mortality, or regrets at experiences that we deprived ourselves of in life for whatever reason, or simply, the paradoxes of life.

Sometimes, we confront life's pertinent questions through the creation of some character. Do we like this character? Would we want to walk their path? If not, am I going down that same path and what can be done to correct it? This type of poetry can be difficult to write and can often require brutal self-honesty and the divulgence of more details pertaining to one's inner workings than what most of us are comfortable with. That said, the rewards make overcoming such misgivings worthwhile. Honest identification and assessment of problems makes them soluble and presenting them through a poem or any other artistic medium makes this possible for both writer and reader. In a way, I consider writing these types of poems an act of service to both myself and the readership.

Other poems in this section are merely about places to which the mind travels and involve no characters of any kind. They are an attempt to present curious questions about the human condition or present human worries and insecurities in a relatable light. These can range from social anxieties to concerns about whether or not one has made good use of this life. Again, I believe these types of poems to be powerful ways of speaking honestly about human issues and affording readers an opportunity to feel heard and understood.

Contradictions

You want it to be read but your book is hidden

You want company but you besiege yourself

You say much but keep it silent

You like the day but live for the night

You want her to burn you but you fear the fire

You want to dip in her ocean but can't swim

You love art but disdain its value

You're surrounded with people but totally alone

Boy are you a man of contradictions

A Final Reckoning

A man of age sits atop a lonely hill

The stars keep watch over his nightly vigil

On some nights he consults the Roman Virgil

On others he plays with a little stone

Wondering how it could have all gone downhill

Why he was sitting every night all on his own

He recalled the great vigor of his youth

When his pack of friends would play by the phone booth

Days would pass with nary a worry

Before self-created devils put him in such a hurry

He loved and was loved

Family stood shoulder to shoulder by his side

But he took for granted and presumed eternal those he loved

One by one they left or died

And he found himself with no one to love

He threw himself into his work in search of fulfillment

Hours and hours vainly stroking his broken pride

And hours and hours more at home with no great sentiment

Only to discover he had been taken for a ride

Atop the lonely hill a realization

That for all he knew he knew nothing at all

He cried tearlessly and wailed silently

And a wintery shiver set in though it was only fall

All his life he thought himself free

But now realized himself to be sentenced to life behind bars

Where he drowned his sorrows hoping all would leave him be

He bought himself jewels, houses, cars and things

Hoping to find contentment in rocks and things

Only to learn happiness cannot be bought with rings

He watched the children play below

And was devoured by the piranhas of envy

Left wondering how he could stoop so low

He recalled his rapid rise through the ranks

The money and adulation with which that came

When he couldn't be stopped by a battalion of tanks

But he learned he had played a losing game

At the end of it all he became weary

And was consumed by thoughts oh so eerie

His brain bombarded duly by thought after thought

"After all, what is this for which I've fought"

Through hard work he came to have everything

Only to realize on that hill that he had nothing

He fashioned himself into a man oh so powerful

Only to be in the end totally powerless

Once t'was all wonderful

But he had come to feel listless

All was aimless, thoughtless, thankless

And as he thought the grip of death grew oh so powerful

The man gazed stupidly at the stars above

Sighed heavily as he beheld the wondrous

And he wondered why he chose a life oh so onerous

He chased houses, cars and rocks and things

When all he needed was a little love

After all, up here he had no things

Just like when he was born, no things

After all this he finally understood

Understood the afflictions of the self

He finally knew well where he stood

And he hated himself

And with that thought he breathed his last

Confessions of a Lonely Introvert

I spend my nights wishing I had the gift of gab

How I wish I could speak like those folks

It's easy for them like opening a new tab

How I wish I could be those folks

Humor? Oh how easily jokes roll off their tongues

Me? Do I even understand it?

Oh how I wish I had their tongues

Boy I would love it

All I want is to be alone

Social gatherings? No thanks

Yet I still want to be thrown a bone

Parties? Thanks but no thanks

Girls? Want their attention as bad as you do

But do I have to be out and about Friday night?

Take a peek or two you know I do

But when it's time to talk I seize in fright

What's so wrong if your BFF's a book

You know I don't want to go to no bar

I'll work late if it'll take me off the hook

Besides, can't even afford a car

I'm in love with solitude

I enjoy my long walks

I don't have an attitude

I just don't enjoy small talks

Yes I do feel misunderstood

A square peg in a round hole

I'm bad at expressing feelings, understood?

And no I'm not an asshole

Yes my demeanor is forlorn

But don't be afraid I don't bite

I've just been a lone soldier since the day I was born

But if I like you, you can enter my world all right

I bumble through speeches so I prefer to write

Thoughts come out clearer via the pen

I know that one day I'll make that right

Not a matter of if but when

I am the lonely introvert

And these are my confessions

To Be a Child Again

How much does it cost Dear Sir to be a child again

To roam the city without a care in the world

There was nothing to worry about then

Every day didn't feel like a trip to the lion's den

What a wonderful world it was! Wonderful world!

What is the price? Name it and I shall pay!

And I shall pay it without delay

It is a request most urgent, a matter most pressing

To have it would be the finest of blessings

How can I be a child again Dear Sir?

What penance shall I perform?

I know the rap sheet contains many sins of mine

I would say anything, fill any form

Where is the dotted line in which I must sign?

What must I do Dear Sir to be a child again?

To run wildly through the forest

To make merry with good friends

To traverse roads freely to their very ends

To be silly and dance the jive

To have the feeling of being alive

What Do I Know

The recurring question plagued my brain again

"What for?" said the still, small voice, "What for?"

"Vanity, vanity, all is vanity, don't you know?"

In the end for all I know, what do I know?

I worked and worked and made good money

Managed to build myself a land of milk and honey

I am rich but I feel poor

I have a house but not a home

Condemned am I to wander like the marauding moor

Safely cocooned am I in my little dome

My dreams are memories of lingering regret

"Why did you not abc, why did you not xyz?"

The whole thing is exhausting as can get

As the bags 'round my eyes show, can't you see?

The recurring question plagued my brain again

"What for?" said the still, small voice, "What for?"

"Vanity, vanity, all is vanity, don't you know?"

In the end, for all I know, what do I know?

I learned today that Hell is one's own creation

That a million hells exist in every nation

In every heart, an abomination that causes desolation

And within, many a cause for consternation

I scream silently for help from above

But streaking across the sky, not one white dove

I cry tearlessly for mercy to the angels above

Misery sure does fit me like a glove

The recurring question plagued my brain again

"What for?" said the still, small voice, "What for?"

"Vanity, vanity, all is vanity, don't you know?"

In the end, for all I know, what do I know?

The Un-valedictorian's Speech

Four years finally happened

Your wits are heavily sharpened

But now it's out to the real world

A mad, mad world

A bad, bad world

Nobody cares if you can integrate or differentiate

They only care if you can dominate

Cuz life's a bitch and everyone needs a hero

No matter if he got a hundred or a zero

This kitchen has very hot heat

If all you know is Shakespeare you're already beat

Here, all you can do is compete

Hung out to dry if you can't stand the heat

Congrats on graduation

But don't think you have it made

Tell me bro how much you gettin' paid

If zero then what's your consolation

Oh that's right

You've got that fifty-grand piece of paper

Damn right

Shout out to every hater

Even if you're goin' hungry

Ten Words

If you had only ten words left to say

What would you say?

Would you say "I love you" to your father

Or to your mother

Would you give your blessing to your son

Or to the sun

Would you expound on The Way

Or that bottle of Chardonnay

Would you confess your love for her

Or pretend you've seen enough of her

Would you tell your secret

Or would you keep the secret

Would you bless the day you were born

Or would you curse it with scorn

If you have only ten words left to say

What would you say?

Perplexed

Never in my history have Ibeen more knowledgeable

But less wise

Never has my life been more palatable

But consumed with thoughts of my demise

Never have I eaten better

But gone hungrier

Never have I smiled wider

But been angrier

I have made my life a contradiction

A mix of sweet and sour

Of paradiso and inferno

What is this juxtaposition

Of which I am the author?

Everything is logical

But nothing makes sense

Everything is possible

But seems so impossible

I am perplexed

I don't understand how to solve this riddle

But I will push on until I have solved the riddle

To Be a Rebel

How bitter is the fruit of your realization?

That you remain stuck in a maze with no exit

I ask if there exists any consolation

If so please do text it

What good is it to die here?

In the end I would still be stuck here

In this incomprehensible show

In the end I must rebel! I must be free!

If I cannot have Nirvana I must create it

A new heaven and a new earth

For the darker recesses of my soul fertile earth

I call for revolution!

A new constitution!

A new code of ethics within!

To be a rebel is to confront the muddle within

To exorcise the demons of ages past

To sympathize with those who came last

To be with conformity aghast

To be a rebel is to conform

Conform to the idea that it's wrong to conform

It means to be alive when you have died

To shake your fist when all others sighed

A Lament

What to do now that all is lost?

By which route do I get lost?

I know now that it's better not to know

I learned today that my glory has brought low

And the fatness seeped from my flesh

Such is the punishment for my idolatry

I have made gods of fleeting things

Of cars, houses, toys and rings

And built altars to them in high places

Which ensnared people of all races

My temple is burning and it shall not be saved

The inhabitants of my Jerusalem raved and raved

I shall return though I know not when

Perhaps my expression will have a haunt to it even then

Appeals

I appeal to you Sisyphus, who rolls the boulder up the hill forevermore

And you too Atlas, who bears the weight of the earth forevermore

And you too Tantalus, whose wishes are so close yet so far forevermore

Look upon us mortals

We pay homage to you

The lives we lead, we mortals

Are a homage to you

To your punishments from the gods

World Government

World government

World government is coming

World government

Big brother's always watching

Serfdom and dungeons and thought police

Fake news and subservient artistry

Fire and brimstone and tattoos and heads flying

No hope or freedom and nowhere to run to it's

World government

World government is coming

World government

Big brother's always watching

Censors and cameras

Jails and informants and watching your every move

War and destruction

False prophet, false peace

Three and a half years of pure hell it's

World government

World government is coming

World government

Big brother's always watching

Black sun and blood moon

Hunger and disease and water gone bitter

Suddenly everything came crashing down

The Great War has started boy it's

World government

World government is coming

World government

Big brother's always watching

Beautiful Despair

You're on the edge of the cliff

It's over if you want it to be

You can play your final riff

And the next day feature on the Daily Bee

A mindless article for a mindless soul

Of another man who has lost his soul

Or you can step back from the precipice

Consign yourself to the hospice

Of a beautiful despair that brings forth light

If you will only put up a fight

You will find the well from which ideas spring

A beautiful despair which fits like a ring

Losing It

Dropped the cup of coffee spilling it all

The trembling hand that held it gave way

Why do I get the feeling that Olympus will fall

And what is this manner in which my heart does beat

And why do I feel a frightening chill in my feet

All these people can they just go away

Any more anxiety and I'll surely lose it all

Every day's commute feels like a visit to the executioner

I will myself up in the morning wishing I hadn't

Every email inches me closer to breaking

Oh how I recall those days in which I was raking

And then how I wish I hadn't

I don't want to remember how far I have fallen

Or how close I am to taking my place among the fallen

I don't want it to be the end

But I feel I can go no further

I type up my plea for help but never hit send

And all can do is mumble "I'm fine"

Unable to take it any further

Because all I see before me is a dead-end street

It takes so much out of me even to it

Laughter bothers and repulses me

I don't understand why the world is laughing at me

What they have going for them that I don't

My eyes beg for help knowing most won't

They can't – they don't understand

They haven't bathed in the darkness

The whole thing is alien to them

And so the suffering continues in silence

Nobody notices or cares to notice

The hero often fails to suppress the violence

The violence existing in the warring mind

He is battle fatigued and asked to soldier on

He will either fall or learn he has won

But at what cost does he fight his war

Life is not life when you're merely existing

Hurtling through this world like rocks through space

None enter the world to be rats running a race

Life was not meant to be inhibiting

It was not meant to be spent fearing Monday

Or the urgent emails on Saturday night

It was meant to be lived!

So the only way out is to live

Live free and live what you love

If the world disapproves oh well

They don't know the heavy price paid to be 'normal'

A life reduced to a routine is not so swell

So my only shot at happiness is to do what I love

And doing this I shall surely live

Down the Bottom of the Well

The water level rises slowly

Where it flows from you're not quite sure

So much protection yet so insecure

For no good reason awash with fear

Fancying yourself among the lonely

There's nothing, but there's something

A phantom that haunts you in the night

A still, small voice bathes you in fear

Until your spirit shivers in fright

And you've become a loathsome little something

But go and tell them all is well

Lie frivolously to your heart's content

Fight your losing battle

And ghosts enter your head free of rent

And you sink to the bottom of the well

These Knots

How many knots exist in you?

Of all colors in the rainbow

Strewn erratically in the table of your life

For when you're flying high or stooping low

Reminders of those times when life cuts like a knife

Keepsakes of the highs that you flew

Colored with the pain of the lows you crawled

Wet with the tears you bawled

And the gentle soak of the morning dew

How entangled are these knots

Just like the ones in your life

So colorful and expressive

Just like the ones in your life

Life is a colorful tangle

Just like these knots before you

The Spaceman

How's life here on Earth?

Place seems rather blue

But thought I'd come ask you

I'd like to know, for what it's worth

Why the funny looks from people?

Do I scare you earthlings?

Fear not, I'm not evil

I'm just not an earthling

I'm the spaceman

Floating about this round blue thing

Which you all refer to as planet Earth

Tell me honestly, is this place just blue in color?

Or is sadness genuine here?

Everyone talks about holding peace near and dear

Yet why do I see neighbors who hate each other?

What are these claims of love for one another?

When some guy got shot down for trying to speak

Is this the freedom of which you speak?

I guess I'll board my tin can and head on back

Life on earth doesn't suit me

Life on Earth the spaceman doesn't see

In fact there's quite a lack

Goodbye earthling

Tell your friends the spaceman sends his regards

Endless Winter

The first snows began to fall

As October died November was born

I had seen the signs of snow to fall

But I was met with scoff and scorn

And suddenly I felt a little older

And suddenly I felt a little colder

November left December came

And the song remained the same

Yeah I bore the weight of falling snow

I kept my pace but felt quite slow

Looking left and right in search of shelter

While trying to relive the summer swelter

With its joys and games I left behind

In search of gold or something of that kind

The old year sailed and the new year docked

And in some cell I sat there trapped and locked

Didn't see its bars, just felt its cold

Running from my brain down through my fingers

Yes the bitter cold sure stays behind and lingers

And sure enough I now felt rather old

As snow fell fast and hard on me

And on this land as far as I could see

Jan becomes the month of love

But there's just this cold I'm captive of

Which hugs and holds me tight within its clutches

14th comes and the duke's left praying for a duchess

As the snow falls ever harder on his shoulders

The stones of ice sure feel like heavy boulders

And he's feeling old and weary

As he contemplates his fate so hard and dreary

March springs forth with its rite of spring

But for me there's destined just one thing

Fighting squalls in search of warmth and shelter

As my bones cry for reprieve from the endless winter

Yes, I perish from the endless winter

April, May and June, come soon

Can't you see I freeze in endless winter?

The snows falls without rest and ever harder

And death looms high above my shoulder

I think of that and feel a little colder

Section Five: Mundane Poems

Introduction

The final section of poems I will present is meant to examine everyday life. Not all the ensuing poetry is celebratory of everyday life; indeed some of it is more devoted to exploring issues and worries with which we would likely be familiar. However, whether the art is celebratory or not, I have often observed that everyday life and everyday problems contain a treasure trove of possible sources of inspiration in spite of them being so often overlooked. This final section of poetry in this collection can therefore be thought of as a kind of expedition into the mundane in hopes of finding within it a nice bounty of treasures.

What are those treasures? I would propose that these would include the ability to highlight and have requisite conversations about our ills that go so ill-perceived (think of the fact that so many of us reduce our lives to a set of predictable routines; to an automation without even realizing it). Our personal dissatisfaction or worries could come to the surface allowing us to meditate on how to solve those issues. On the more positive side, simple appreciation of the beauty of human existence and its challenges can provide the soul with much needed refreshment. This could take the form of laughing at ourselves by seeing the humor in everyday life. Okay, enough discussion. Shall we go treasure hunting?

Rat Racing

The rats do run in an endless loop

It's spin and spin for you and me

Run and run for she and he

Rats racing by group by group

They hustle and bustle hoping for freedom

An illusory life forty years in the making

But all that exists is their hermit kingdom

A far-flung corner in an office of cubicles

Monday comes so fast and Friday comes so slow

And you spend your days feeling low

All that study and all that work

Did you really do it all for a routine?

You look left and right and there's no way out

So you get all mad and pout

Hope's a word you find offensive

That's cuz life's got you on the defensive

You'd love nothing more than to do what you love

But bills gotta be paid and you ain't got nothing saved

So misery fits you like a glove

Instead of being able to sleep you've ranted and raved

The world's falling apart for you

You've realized you're rat racing

And you can't see a way out

Leaving you wishing for the end to come

You just hate your life that much

Cuz you're going in circles you don't see an off-ramp

Every email in your inbox is an act of terror

Every second the noose gets tighter

And no matter what the load feels no lighter

Shivering in terror you make the fatal error

You take whatever feels good to numb the pain

Whatever will make the sun come out

In this mad world of eternal rain

You tune right in and you drop right out

Your miserable devil you

You thought you would live the dream

But here in the nightmare are you

Rats racing to and fro as you hopelessly scream

And then it's over

Either the trap door finally opened

Or you expired from racing

What is this pain you're facing

The aches and pains from years of racing

Rat racing to Armageddon

Sketches of Everyday Life

1. <u>Waking Up and Off to Work</u>

Six o'clock alarm rings loud

You let out a big ol' roar

Long, tall 'n' proud

Feelin' like you're ready to soar

But then the night of tossin' 'n' turnin' sets in

And your legs begin to feel like jelly

And ya need to get a somethin' in that belly

You brush your teeth 'n' comb your hair

In the end you look no worse for the wear

A few bites into that English muffin 'n' egg

And through the door sticks out the first leg

Off you go! Time to work!

2. The Train Ride

It's seven thirty and before you, a sea of people

Hear the distant rumble of an approaching train

Frowns dotting the landscape are perhaps a prequel

Of the day that lies ahead

By the end you'll feel all dead, all dead

Here comes the morning train

Doors open and all manner of humanity enter

People of all ages, faces and races

All off to the nowhere bound daily races

A million Sisyphuses ready to push their rocks

Each with a few minutes to savor their penuries

Keeping their feelings under the tightest of locks

They marinate deliciously in their daily miseries

3. Arriving at Work

The train ride ends with a sense of wonder and dread

Barely eight but you're already feelin' dead

A wondrous blue light emanates from your left pocket

Your phone beckons for your attention

You reach for it as your body recoils in tension

1313 UNREAD EMAILS!

Shivering, you return the joey to its pouch

And you keep trudging along slowly

As some crazy person shouts some tall tales

You reach the office and skulk inside

Every minute trickles by sooooo sloooowwwlllly

This day ain't gonna be no rainbow ride

4. The Office

Tiki-Taka sings the keyboard

You're not so sure you like its tune

Ten and you wish your life hummed to a different tune

By eleven you're numbingly bored

Noon and you go for lunch if you can

Shoot the shit with Joe, Tim and Dan

At one it's time to type your tuneless tunes again

Two, three, four p.m. and the song remains the same

Five and your stomach frets over dinner

Six and you're so tired you forgot your name

Time to go and you feel like a winner

Tomorrow you do it all over again

5. Going Home

6.10 train packed to the rafters

You bob 'n' weave 'n' push 'n' squeeze

Gotta get in – there ain't no morning after

Huh?!… A delay? Puh-leasssee!

Nuthin' to do, just sit 'n' wait

Finally – train is in movement

Then comes the bus ride that you hate

Because that's time to think

And thinking hurts more than dying to you

You get home 'n' not much in the fridge

With what you have make due

6. Dinner

Cue the evenin' growls

Off to the kitchen with all that you need

Healthy stuff only for diet advice thou shalt heed

As you cuttingly contemplate the hootin' owls

Which watch from afar as you slave away

And it cuts like a knife

Cuz you know you're puttin' on a borin' show

But what do you care? Dinner's ready anyway

Plop it down on the table below

And have a little life in your life

7. Winding Down the Hours

The sofa beckons for the warmth of your tuchus

Favorite show's 'bout to come on

Gotta find out how it ends for Fanny 'n' Don

And bring your phone so you live-tweet the ruckus

Reality TV's all too real for you after all

And when watchin' many a tear has to fall

In between the misty glances at the clock

As you passively watch time pass

You discover Don's a bit of an ass

And that for many Fanny preens

And is there life in those screens?

8. Sleep

Plop on down champ!

T'is the sweetest part of the day

Settle down 'n' turn of the lamp

Sleep your sorrows away

Dream dreams if you can

Wake up from nightmares if you must

Your eyes are flickering weakly

And on your bed you collapse meekly

In a flash you finally go bust

You driftin' off – so long Marianne!

You can face tomorrow when it comes

It's just another day

Nothing Comes to Mind

I scribble the odd thing here and there

But I seem to go nowhere

No real clue now what comes next

No clear ideas on my mind

That could be turned to text

No clue now how to get 'round the bind

Scribble, scribble

Wiggle, wiggle

Nothing comes to mind

It's due tomorrow and I'm fallin' quite behind

Try to think of heroes from the past

And of what I published last

Maybe clues will come from there

Other things'll be brought to bear

And I can beat the clock

Tick, tock, tick, tock

Scribble, scribble

Wiggle, wiggle

Nothing comes to mind

It's due tomorrow and I'm fallin' quite behind

Tryin' to think outside the box

You know I'd work hard as an ox

But I'm stuck down here and nowhere near

To knowing what comes next

Gonna get kicked in the rear

If I put nothing to text

Scribble, scribble

Wiggle, wiggle

Nothing comes to mind

It's due tomorrow and I'm fallin' quite behind

Help!

I don't know what to write!

Another Day at the Races

Six a.m. the alarm rings

Get on up

Put on your things

Have your meal

Brush your teeth

Check your email

What's the deal

Gotta run

Meeting at nine a.m.

Already late

Train's delayed

Ain't fun to be on the run

Meet at nine

It doesn't go okay

Nasty stares for being late

Takeaways and other things

Lunch'll have to wait

But you'll be fine

Five p.m. comes and still at work

Going to OT once again

Plug away and eat a snack

Finally you get on up

Finally you've done your work

You hop on the train

On legs barely your own

Then you fall in bed

Too tired to hear the rain

Tomorrow you'll do it again

Another day at the races

And then the next day again

Portrait of a Racing Mind

Forgot to take out the trash

Status report's due today

Wait! Your lunch

Oh, hey! An idea for a poem

Bah, no time to write

Mom's birthday present!

Too late – t'was yesterday

Ah! Before I forget…

Um… I forgot

Yes! Financials data due at noon

My poem?

Uh… rats! Idea vanished

Status deck looks good

Oh, and does she love me?

And by the way, are aliens real?

Nonsense! Back to work!

Wait! I'm at home?

Time to sleep

Toss 'n' turn

I have a dream!

Shut up!

Nope, I did not exercise

Er, is it pay day today?

Paper! I have an idea for a story

Or did I?

The Wandering Poet

Five p.m. and he hustles out of work

His appointment with the pavement awaits

There are no pre-planned dates

Just wants to get his legs a little work

The cold gently plays on his cheeks

The flashing lights of the city tickle his eyes

Smells flatter and offend his nose in turns

And with the scanning movement of his eyes

He searches for a flashing light of inspiration

Where and if it will appear he doesn't know

If it will come from way up high or from way down low

As his forehead is gently dabbed with perspiration

As he trots along hands in pocket

He hears the raving of a lunatic

Hums his distorted version of the street musician's tune

Not caring if strangers fancy him a loon

And as he contemplates the graffiti on the wall

And the anger that inspired it all

He begins to feel a life in his life

An intimate connection to forces yet unknown

With every pace he learns the city

Becomes one with the hustle and bustle

Sneaks a peek at a girl sitting pretty

In the dance studio of one Mrs. Fussell

Picks up bits and pieces of twenty languages

Which he may or may not use in verse

And then he passes a lodge

Which offers secrets to the universe

He passes the library as many do their learning

Beside a gentleman's club full of passions burning

A gym bustles with those educating their bodies

And inside a small cafe the idle chatter of lovers in love

On the sidewalk folks sit doing nothing at all

And while all is seen by a lonely dove

Addicts sharply penetrate their bodies

Knowing that one day Olympus must surely fall

And so Ulysses finishes his Odyssey

He has seen all that the poet must see

Words begin to order themselves in his mind

And on a piece of paper he must respond in kind

Afterword

And so ends my first artistic offering to you all. I hope it was enlightening and stupefying, uplifting and infuriating, funny and serious, happy and sad. I hope it took you on a journey through as much of the human experience as is possible within the confines of one modest collection of poetry from an unknown, solitary voice crying out in the concrete wilderness. I also hope that this work is a source of comfort in this trying and uncertain time of human history. Most of all however, I hope that this collection is your own inspiration to proceed with committing whatever ideas currently kick about in your head to paper. I look forward to coming into contact with these ideas of yours.

Now let us revisit the question 'what is poetry?'. I view it in the following manner. Poetry is evidence of life. It is a signal propagating through space, bouncing off of the planets, comets, the sun and the stars to carry evidence of your existence to the universe. Art in general can be viewed in this manner. Poetry is also another thing. It is an exercise in nostalgia as is any other art form. Art to a certain degree is the ashes of those burnt out, impossible dreams of old that we stubbornly cling to. It is all those things that we wanted to be, the love we wanted to make, the tales that kicked about in our heads; a prayer for the return of simpler, more innocent times. Art is the altar we keep to the familiar spirits in our minds!

Lastly, a few rules for writing. First of all, do not force it. The urge comes suddenly and writing as such a bulb goes off feels natural and fluid. I have learned through this journey to allow my brain to rest and focus on other things. There are days where all you will have for such efforts is a few passages of which you will be rather dismayed. Do not allow this to dishearten you. Do not discard these literary abortions either. Revisiting them later may cause the proverbial lightbulb to switch back on. Maybe it will be one sentence or even just a single word.

My second admonition is to closely observe the world around you. This means being aware of world events but also of your immediate surroundings. You may find a source of inspiration there. It may come in the ravings of a lunatic, an off-hand quip from a friend, an anecdote from a co-worker etc. The point is that your source of inspiration need not be anything cataclysmic or especially strange. Ordinary life can hold within it just as many if not more sources of inspiration. That is why so many of the masters have found within the mundane a magic well of ideas with which to fuel their writing.

Finally, be sure to play around and try some things. Know the rules but do not be afraid to break them. Progress in art does not come from blind obedience to existing norms but from questioning them. Art advances through the exploration of new frontiers. This requires bravery and this requires open mindedness, therefore I admonish you to be both brave and open minded. Look for inspirations in unexpected places. Look for ideas in unexpected places. Also, look for it in places that scare you. Usually, this will be somewhere within. Remember that the writer reaches into his own darkness and from within it pulls out light. The light cannot be pulled out before reaching into the darkness. This requires bravery. This requires the willingness to go against convention.

The above admonitions can be summarized into one: look for sources of inspiration. Inspiration is the fuel by which creative journeys can be undertaken and continued. To keep flying through the skies of imagination requires the fuel of inspiration. Otherwise, expect to crash down to earth in a most ignominious way. Be courageous in your creative journey. Be tenacious in your creative journey.

But above all, enjoy the creative journey. Our lives are but tiny slivers in the long timeline of human history and it is our duty to make of those tiny slivers as much as we can and leave this earth without regrets and with all our artistry bequeathed to those who will come after us. With that thought I shall leave you for now, until the muse should visit me again with new verbal manipulations to share with my fellow man.